Turn the next two pages and see just
how big an alligator snapping turtle can be.

![Jim Arnosky's](author portrait)

Jim Arnosky's
ALL ABOUT Turtles

SCHOLASTIC

New York   Toronto   London   Auckland   Sydney
Mexico City   New Delhi   Hong Kong   Buenos Aires

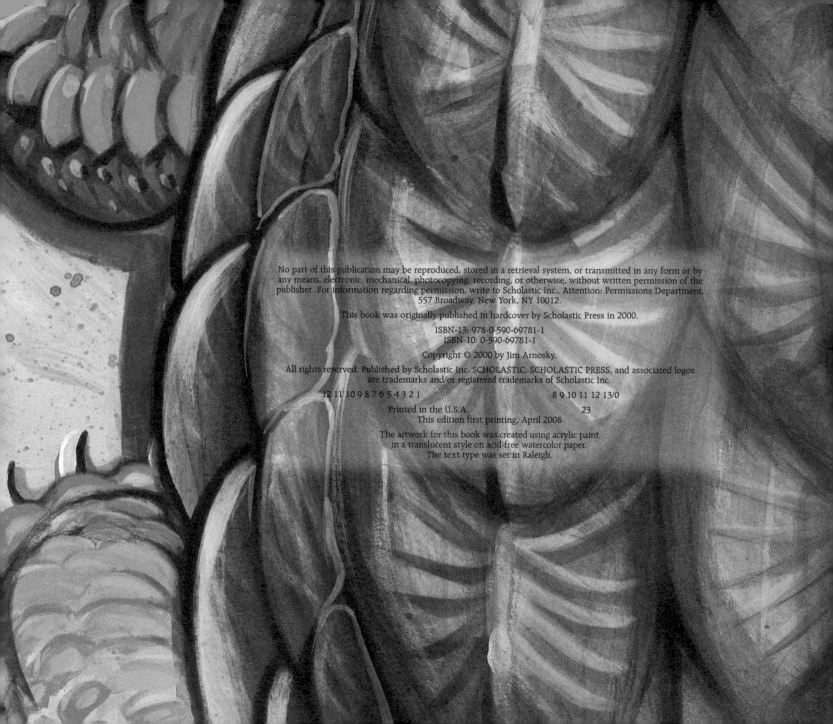

This book was originally published in hardcover by Scholastic Press in 2000.

ISBN-13: 978-0-590-69781-1
ISBN-10: 0-590-69781-1

Copyright © 2000 by Jim Arnosky.

12 11 10 9 8 7 6 5 4 3 2 1   8 9 10 11 12 13/0

Printed in the U.S.A.   23
This edition first printing, April 2008

The artwork for this book was created using acrylic paint in a translucent style on acid-free watercolor paper. The text type was set in Raleigh.

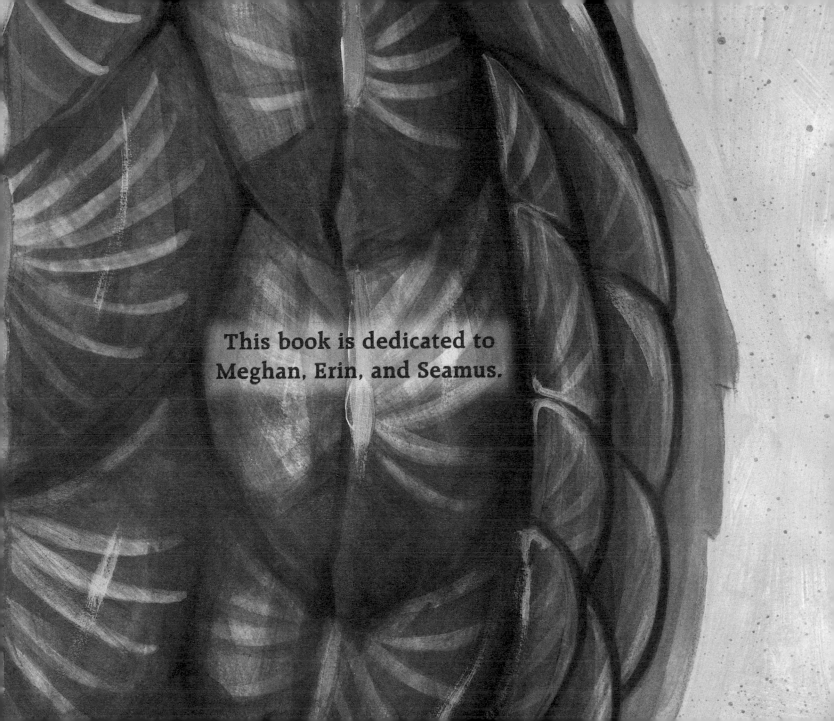

This book is dedicated to
Meghan, Erin, and Seamus.

Have you ever wondered about turtles?
How many kinds of turtles are there?
Why do turtles have shells?
What do turtles eat?
How old can turtles live to be?

This book answers all these questions and more.
It's all about turtles!

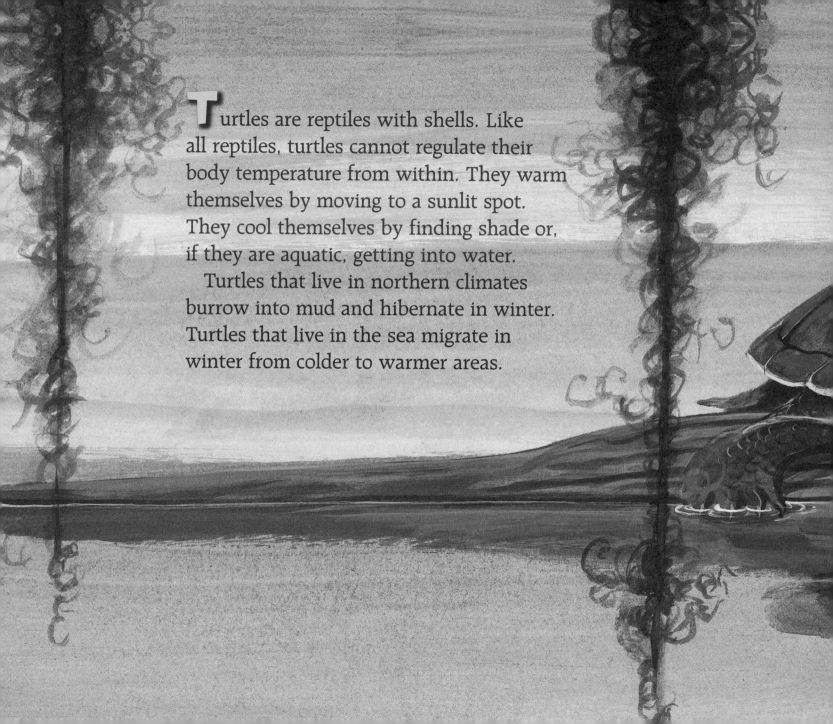

Turtles are reptiles with shells. Like all reptiles, turtles cannot regulate their body temperature from within. They warm themselves by moving to a sunlit spot. They cool themselves by finding shade or, if they are aquatic, getting into water.

Turtles that live in northern climates burrow into mud and hibernate in winter. Turtles that live in the sea migrate in winter from colder to warmer areas.

Red-bellied turtle
sunning itself on a log

cooter

Worldwide, there are more than two hundred species of turtles. All turtles fall into these groups: freshwater turtles, saltwater turtles, and land-dwelling turtles.

The cooter, spotted turtle, and painted turtle are all small freshwater turtles. They are almost entirely aquatic.

painted turtle

box turtle

spotted turtle

Box turtles are land-dwelling turtles with hinged bottom shells that can close tightly.

desert tortoise

wood turtle

Wood turtles and terrapins look similar but are different types of turtles. Both spend as much time in water as they do on land.

diamondback terrapin

Tortoises are exclusively land-dwelling.

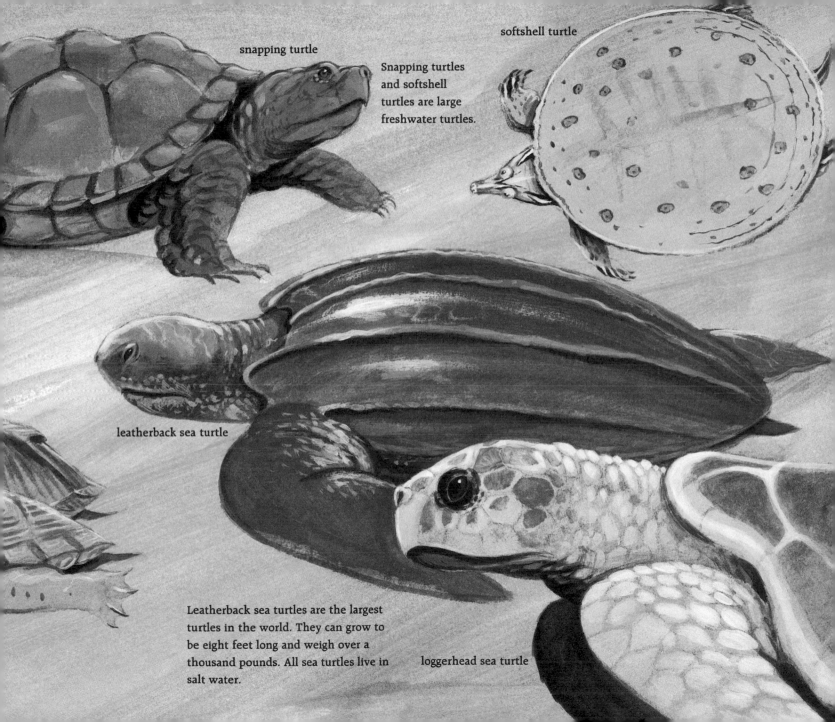

snapping turtle

Snapping turtles
and softshell
turtles are large
freshwater turtles.

softshell turtle

leatherback sea turtle

Leatherback sea turtles are the largest
turtles in the world. They can grow to
be eight feet long and weigh over a
thousand pounds. All sea turtles live in
salt water.

loggerhead sea turtle

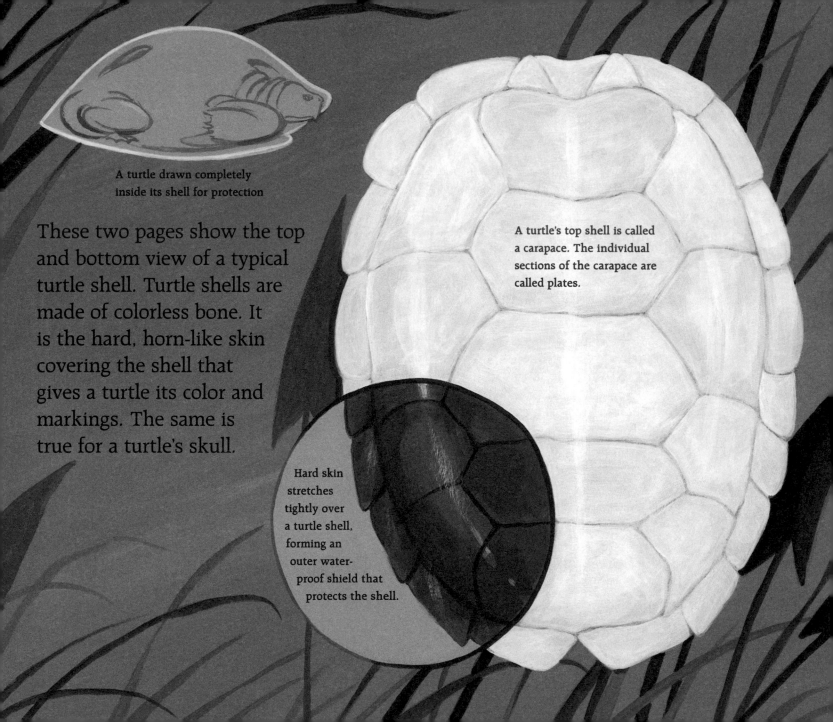

A turtle drawn completely
inside its shell for protection

These two pages show the top
and bottom view of a typical
turtle shell. Turtle shells are
made of colorless bone. It
is the hard, horn-like skin
covering the shell that
gives a turtle its color and
markings. The same is
true for a turtle's skull.

A turtle's top shell is called
a carapace. The individual
sections of the carapace are
called plates.

Hard skin
stretches
tightly over
a turtle shell,
forming an
outer water-
proof shield that
protects the shell.

A female turtle's plastron is convex.

Male turtles have concave plastrons.

Depending on the turtle species, the bottom shell will be small, like the one shown here, or large enough to cover the entire bottom area of the turtle.

A turtle's bottom shell is called a plastron.

Turtle skull showing large eye sockets, big, powerful jaw, and sharply hooked beak. Turtles have no teeth.

The huge shell of a sea turtle is actually thin and lightweight in proportion to the turtle's heavy body. The large front flippers and muscular neck of a sea turtle cannot be drawn inside the shell.

loggerhead sea turtle

Sea turtles have flippers instead of legs. The long and powerful front flippers are used to paddle swiftly through the water. The wide hind flippers act as rudders for steering.

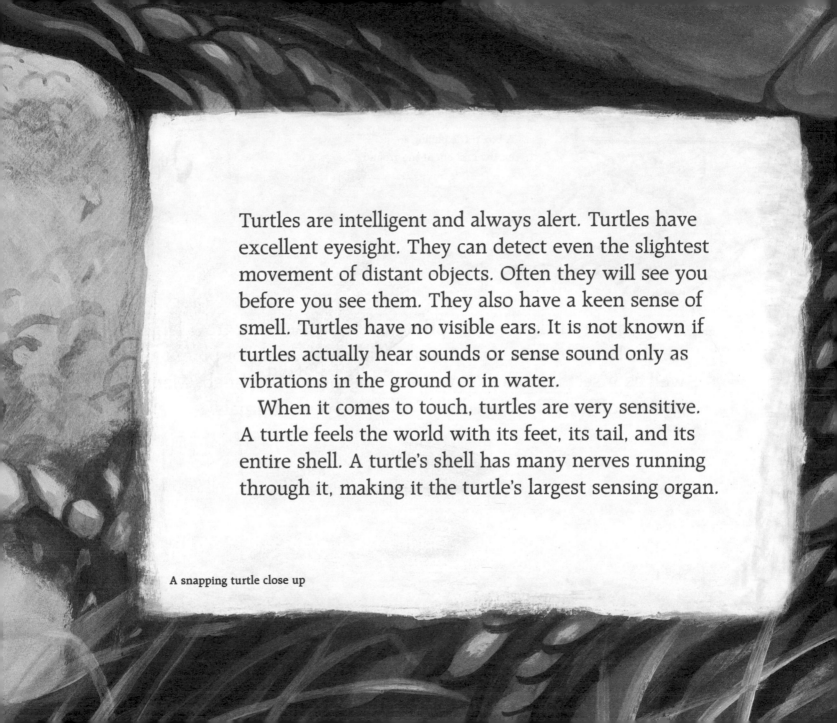

Turtles are intelligent and always alert. Turtles have excellent eyesight. They can detect even the slightest movement of distant objects. Often they will see you before you see them. They also have a keen sense of smell. Turtles have no visible ears. It is not known if turtles actually hear sounds or sense sound only as vibrations in the ground or in water.

When it comes to touch, turtles are very sensitive. A turtle feels the world with its feet, its tail, and its entire shell. A turtle's shell has many nerves running through it, making it the turtle's largest sensing organ.

A snapping turtle close up

A box turtle pulling an
earthworm out of the ground

Very young turtles feed mostly on insects. As they grow larger,
turtles become more omnivorous, eating a variety of plants as
well as insects, mollusks, worms, crustaceans, and fish. Many
species of turtles will even eat carrion—dead animals.

A painted turtle feeding on mayflies

jellyfish

Sea turtles will eat eel grass, crabs, conches, clams, oysters, fish, sponges, and even jellyfish. Snapping turtles eat anything they can catch, from fish to floating ducks.

The alligator snapping turtle lures fish into its gaping mouth by wiggling the tiny, pink, worm-like tip of its tongue.

The least predatory of all turtles are the tortoises. These shy, burrow-digging turtles feed almost exclusively on plants. The only tortoises that live in the United States are the gopher tortoises.

Gopher tortoises share their burrows with other animals, including rattlesnakes. Wherever you see a gopher tortoise, you must take care and watch all around. The tortoise could have a rattlesnake for a roommate!

gopher tortoise

diamondback rattlesnake

Female sea turtles come to land only to lay their eggs. Male sea turtles never come ashore.

All turtles reproduce in the same way. Some time after mating with a male, the female turtle digs a nest hole into which she deposits her eggs. The number of eggs varies from one to one hundred and thirty, depending on the turtle species. After laying all her eggs, the turtle covers the nest hole with loose soil and then abandons it. The sun-warmed earth, not the turtle mother, incubates the turtle eggs.

Cross-section drawing showing a green sea turtle laying eggs in her freshly dug nest hole

Turtle eggs are round, white, and soft. The size of the egg depends on the species of turtle. These eggs are shown actual size.

sea turtle egg

snapping turtle egg

painted turtle egg

Turtle eggshells and raccoon tracks

Not all turtle eggs get a chance to develop fully. Many are sniffed out and eaten by raccoons and other predators.

Egg-eating predators cannot find every turtle nest. Lots of baby turtles do hatch and dig their way up out of the ground.

Hatchling turtles may go directly to the nearest water, where they are less vulnerable to attacks by shore birds. Or, if the hatchlings are a land-loving species of turtle, they may hurry to the safety of woodland or brush, where they can hide amid the leaf litter on the ground.

Here are five distinctly different species of baby turtles, shown a little larger than actual size so you can see their individual shell patterns.

snapping turtle

painted turtle

green sea turtle

red-eared turtle

box turtle

With only their shells to protect them, baby turtles have been making the perilous journey from nest hole to habitat since the days of the dinosaurs.

Turtles live long lives. Some species live to be more than one hundred years old. But even a day-old turtle knows its way in the world.

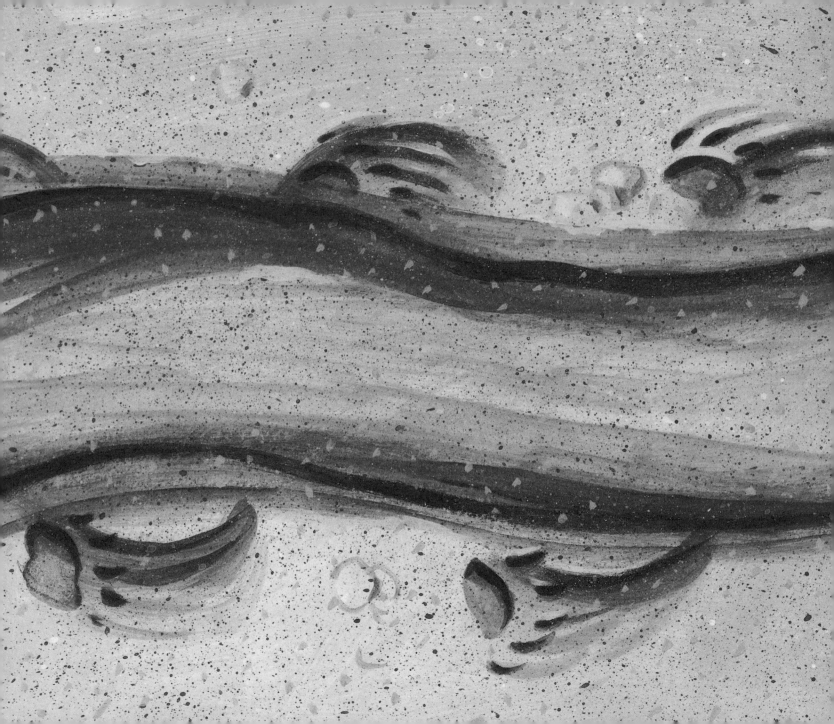

Michelle Sherburne

MEET JIM ARNOSKY

Jim Arnosky is the author and illustrator of nearly 100 books about wildlife and nature for children. He has received numerous honors for his work, including the American Association for the Advancement of Science Lifetime Achievement Award for excellence in science illustration.

Jim has spent many years observing and learning about turtles in their native habitats. He based every illustration in this book on turtles and locations he actually saw.

When he is not traveling to visit schools and explore nature, Jim Arnosky lives in Vermont, with his wife, Deanna.